IN

CW00552735

Stru

Pope Francis has a deep devotion to the Blessed Mother and to what is perhaps the most popular way of praying with her: the Rosary.

Those circlets of beads, with their repetitions of familiar prayers, are, he says, a great weapon in the struggles we face daily in our faith. They bind us to the Blessed Mother in her own struggles to accept the role God had called her to as the Mother of the Savior—a woman whose heart would be pierced often as people rejected her Son, convicted him as a common criminal, and executed him. They also bind us to her in the joy of the resurrection, when all the promises God made to her were fulfilled. And, says Pope Francis, they bind us to her in hope— hope that our prayers will also be heard when we reach out to God in our need.

With Pope Francis' words to guide us, let us reflect on and pray the mysteries of the Rosary, trusting that Mary will lead us more deeply into the life, death, and resurrection of her Son.

The quotes from Pope Francis were chosen
by Deborah McCann, who also wrote the reflections
and the "Ponder" and "Pray" pieces.

Cover photo: Stefano Spaziani

ISBN 978-1-62785-150-3 ■ Printed in the U.S.A.

The
Joyful
Mysteries

1 | THE ANNUNCIATION

If we do not lower ourselves, we are not Christian.

It's hard to imagine a "lowering" more profound than that of God coming to earth as a human being, taking on our form and nature. More than that, to pick a young, unmarried woman from an insignificant town to be the bearer of his Son seems the height of absurdity. Yet it was this girl still in her teens, bethrothed but not yet married to her fiancé, whom God chose, confident that she was worthy of the task, in spite of any ridicule or suspicion that would surround her pregnancy. Indeed, as Pope Francis points out, our primary call as disciples is to lower ourselves so that we may be of service to others, no matter the cost. God's example is ours, and Mary's assent is our path to follow.

PONDER
How willing am I to offer up everything in service to God?

PRAY
Mary, give me your bravery in all that I do.

2 | THE VISITATION

*This is the song of those who have faced the struggle
of life while holding on to hope.*

Two moments stand out in the account of Mary visiting Elizabeth. First, the child in Elizabeth's womb, aware of the identity of Mary's child, leaps when Mary arrives. And Mary sings a wondrous and humbly triumphant song of praise to God: the Magnificat. Pope Francis says that this song is OUR song: the song of the saints. Some of these saints, he says, we know well. Others are known only to God, but we meet them daily: moms and dads and grandparents and teachers and public servants and lay ministers and priests and sisters...and children. We are all part of this song of hope. In this encounter it is clear that "the little people" matter greatly to God. God does not forget us!

PONDER

How authentic is my praise for God's goodness?

PRAY

Elizabeth, help me to recognize the saviors in my midst.

3 | THE NATIVITY

God became a child to reach out to us
through his love, humility, and poverty.

The mystery of the Incarnation, says Pope Francis, is that God chose to come to us to share completely in our lives. He didn't just make an appearance or announce his presence with some grandiose miracle. Rather, he came as one of the most humble, helpless creatures: a human baby. Pope Francis reminds us that, by choosing to come among us in this way, God shows us how we are to be for one another: open, vulnerable, and innocent. This flies in the face of how we think we should be: powerful, wary, and crafty. But Jesus' model of "simplicity, humility, and meekness" is what we are asked to follow.

PONDER

How does innocence still inform my life?

PRAY

Holy Infant, help me to trust in the power of goodness
and humility to guide my life.

4 | THE PRESENTATION IN THE TEMPLE

Let us be led by the Spirit,
who always invites us to joy.

Forty days after Jesus' birth, Mary and Joseph bring him to the temple. And there they have a profoundly moving encounter with the aged Simeon and Anna—two people who have lived their lives serving God and who are now over-joyed to meet their Savior in the form of this little baby. This is, Pope Francis tells us, a remarkable encounter of "observance with prophecy," of the young family with wise elders—a true act of the Holy Spirit. To be open to the Spirit in every en-counter of our lives—not being rigid or close-minded, but open to the possibility of meeting God face to face—is a wonderful gift!

PONDER

How open am I to the wisdom of others, especially from those from whom I least expect it?

PRAY

Simeon and Anna, keep me open to the wisdom
you share!

5 | THE FINDING OF THE CHILD JESUS IN THE TEMPLE

Be protectors of God's gifts!

When contemplating this all-too-human story of parental fear, disbelief, anguish, and then joy, Pope Francis concentrates on the role of Joseph as protector of his family. Throughout his life, Joseph remained the faithful partner and the guiding influence for Jesus, and the steady role model families need. Pope Francis uses this mystery to remind us of our need to protect one another—husbands and wives protecting each other, parents protecting children, children protecting parents, and all of us protecting our world. In this picture of the Holy Family, we see our own call revealed clearly.

PONDER
Am I a good protector of those I love?

PRAY
Joseph, help me to follow your example of steady, patient care for others.

The
Luminous
Mysteries

1 | THE BAPTISM IN THE JORDAN

*Let us allow ourselves to be invaded by the love
of God. This is the great time of mercy!*

At Jesus' birth, the heavens were opened. And
it is with the gifts of the Holy Spirit that we receive at baptism that we ourselves begin to un-
derstand what that means. Sin had closed the
heavens, Pope Francis says, but God's love is so
great that he tore the heavens open with the
gift of his Son, inaugurating the age of mercy
that is still with us. As we ponder Jesus humbling
himself to be baptized, and as we reflect on the
words of the Father—"This is my beloved Son,
with whom I am well pleased"—let us remember
that these words are meant for us as well, as we
ask the Spirit to fill our hearts with God's love so
that we may love one another.

PONDER

What has my baptism truly meant in my life?

PRAY

Holy Spirit, fill me with the awareness of your love!

2 | THE WEDDING AT CANA

*What happened at the wedding feast of Cana
happens at every wedding—if we realize it!*

In a wedding homily, Pope Francis talked about the
wedding feast at Cana, where Jesus made his first public
sign of his coming ministry. How easy it is, Pope Francis
says, to get caught up in all the externals of a wedding:
the dress, the decorations, the reception. This is not
wrong, he continues, IF the bride and groom are aware
of the deeper purpose of what these externals reveal:
the couple's awareness that "it is the presence of the
Lord that will render your marriage full and profoundly
true." "The best for last" may not be fully revealed until
a couple has lived a faith-filled and faithful love for de-
cades—but what a witness such love reveals!

PONDER

Am I aware of God's presence in my loving
relationships?

PRAY

*Lord, help me to keep deepening my love
for others and for you.*

3 | THE PROCLAMATION
OF THE KINGDOM

*The highest compliment you can receive is that
you are a worker for the kingdom.*

When Jesus' disciples returned happy from their evangelizing missions, Pope Francis says, Jesus invited them to go off with him to pray and refresh themselves. But he did not shower them with compliments or offer new strategies for more effective results. What he said to them was that they should tell themselves that in everything they were "useless servants." To say this meant that they were not following their own path, but that of Jesus, who came to show the way of discipleship. We proclaim the kingdom much more by how we act than by what we say. How do we proclaim the kingdom in our daily lives?

PONDER

How can I better serve God?

PRAY

Jesus, keep me humble and focused on your path!

4 | THE TRANSFIGURATION

The intimate encounter with God on the
mountaintop pushes us back down to meet
the needs of our brothers and sisters.

Moments of connecting with God in prayer, Pope Francis tells us, are crucial to our healthy witness. But we can't stop there—this grace is not given to us to be hoarded, but to be shared. Yes, we need to go off by ourselves to center ourselves and discern the voice of the Lord, but that encounter must lead to our becoming ever more aware of the needs of our neighbors—those who are tired, hungry, lost, broken, and afraid. But once we have truly felt the Lord's goodness, helping our neighbors will be a joyful task, one we can embrace wholeheartedly.

PONDER

How aware am I of God's voice in my life?

PRAY

Transfigured Lord, help me share your light with all!

5 | THE INSTITUTION OF THE EUCHARIST

Jesus made himself our servant.
We must be servants to one another.

Over and over again Pope Francis stresses the servant-hood of Jesus. In a homily on Holy Thursday, he talked about how this sacrificing of ourselves for others is the hallmark of our Christian witness. And Jesus' actions are rooted in his love for us, the same love we are to have for one another. In this homily the pope did not talk about the bread and wine of our eucharistic feast. Before we can share the banquet, he said, we must wash one another's feet—the gesture a slave makes for guests of the household. In this way, the pope drives home the image of a God whose life was devoted to service of others, expressed so poignantly in this humble action. We who are his body here on earth are asked to do the same.

PONDER

How much am I a servant, and how much a master?

PRAY

Servant Lord, fill me with your humility.

The
Sorrowful
Mysteries

1 | THE AGONY IN THE GARDEN

Who am I before the sufferings of my Lord?

As a Jesuit, Pope Francis is familiar with the tradition of St. Ignatius' Spiritual Exercises, where the retreatant is asked to ponder the gospel stories "from the inside," as it were, imagining oneself as part of the story with the crowds, disciples, and others. Here, with the mystery of Jesus at prayer in the Garden of Gethsemane, Pope Francis asks us to ponder where we stand while Jesus prays in his torment: Are we the ones asleep like the disciples he took with him? Are we those who are about to run away? Or are we ready to stand by his side, as did his mother and the disciple he loved? It's well worth pondering, especially when we're praying for people who themselves are suffering.

PONDER

Where do I stand when praying for those who are suffering—alongside or at a distance?

PRAY

Lord, strengthen me so that I will never abandon you!

2 | THE SCOURGING AT THE PILLAR

"Father, I have saved your children with these wounds."

Pope Francis imagines Jesus appearing before his Father in heaven, still carrying the wounds of his scourging and his crucifixion, and he imagines him telling his Father that this is how he paid the price for our sins. Pope Francis says that this is how Jesus advocates for us and prays for our protection. How immense is that sacrifice that redeemed us and made us worthy of eternal life! And how gentle and humble is that prayer—to ask the Father's protection for those whose sins caused his death! How many ways do we torture each other—and ourselves—with pettiness and gossip and dismissiveness? How can we relieve pain instead of causing it?

PONDER

How have I caused others pain?

PRAY

Wounded Lord, there are some wounds only you can heal. Please heal us and help us not to wound each other!

3 | THE CROWNING WITH THORNS

Torture is a very grave sin.

It's easy to get caught up in the story of Jesus' passion and death and condemn the methods the Roman soldiers used to humiliate and ridicule him. The crown of thorns is a particularly brutal insult. But have we improved at all as human beings in the way we treat others, even sometimes considering them less than human? Pope Francis has harsh words for those who practice torture of any kind, calling it a mortal sin. Brought down to our own day-to-day level, how do we work for human rights and dignity so that no one need suffer physical or mental torture—that of brutality, or displacement, or rejection? How can the image of Jesus crowned with thorns redouble our resolve to heal others?

PONDER
Who is suffering that I haven't noticed?

PRAY
Jesus, crowned with thorns but with eyes full
of compassion, heal my ignorance and open my eyes.

4 | THE CARRYING OF THE CROSS

The cross of Christ teaches us about love.

In addressing this mystery of the Rosary, Pope Francis says that the cross that Jesus carried should open our eyes to how much we are loved, and what the enormity of that love asks of us in return. He asks us to consider how many people were a part of that journey to Calvary—Pilate, who didn't have the courage of his convictions; Simon of Cyrene, who helped him shoulder the burden; Mary and the other women, who accompanied him all the way—and to figure out for ourselves whom we most resemble. If we allow ourselves to be affected by the cross, we can begin to notice and to reach out in mercy and love to all who need our help. The cross is a lesson of love.

PONDER

Who am I like on Jesus' path? Who would I want to be?

PRAY

*Jesus, let your cross transform me to shoulder
the burdens of all those you love—everyone!*

5 | THE CRUCIFIXION

*On the cross, Jesus unites himself to all victims
of all kinds of violence.*

In a Good Friday message, Pope Francis spoke of how
Christ's sacrifice on the cross united Christ with all those
who suffer violence in silence—victims of torture, perse-
cution, ostracism, addiction, and those who suffer from
hunger in the midst of plenty. All of Pope Francis' mes-
sages of mercy and service and stewardship come down
to this mystery of the cross and God's great love for us
that even death cannot overcome. How will we work to
express our gratitude? By working ourselves to relieve
the sufferings of others, by giving voice to the voiceless,
and by taking steps to help all live in dignity and peace.

PONDER

What organizations exist in my own community to
help the homeless, the hungry, or the addicted? How
can I offer my help?

PRAY

*Good Thief, may my eyes be opened like yours
to recognize my Savior!*

The
Glorious
Mysteries

1] THE RESURRECTION OF THE LORD

2] THE ASCENSION INTO HEAVEN

3] THE DESCENT OF THE HOLY SPIRIT

4] THE ASSUMPTION OF MARY

5] THE CORONATION OF MARY

1 | THE RESURRECTION

Let us ask ourselves the angel's question:
"Why do you seek the living among the dead?"

"Opening the horizons of joy and hope" and "coming out of our spaces of sadness" are the images Pope Francis uses to celebrate the Easter mystery of Christ's resurrection from the dead. How often, he says, we get caught up in all that deprives us of the important things of life, that can deaden our spirit, when what we need to do is to seek the Lord where he may be found— in our hearts, in the faces of those around us, in prayer both personal and communal, and in the mission before us to share that good news. Our call is to bring this light to others, and resurrection joy will give us the grace to do so.

PONDER

How quick am I to be transformed by joy?

PRAY

Resurrected Lord, fill me with your light so that I may bring your life to others!

2 | THE ASCENSION

In Christ our humanity was taken to God.

The first disciples had so much and yet so little to work with in their mission. They had Jesus with them throughout his ministry, and then they were privileged to witness him after his resurrection. But when Jesus ascended into heaven forty days after Easter, they were left alone looking up into heaven confused and afraid. The Holy Spirit had yet to descend and fill them with courage and assurance. We are so fortunate, Pope Francis says, because we know we have Jesus as our Advocate. He is our constant guide, pulling us ever onward like a mountain-climbing guide. And there is more: when Jesus ascended, the pope says, he took our humanity to the Father—thereby not only redeeming us but ennobling us in God's sight. Jesus is vouching for us—we're in good hands!

PONDER

Do I rely on Jesus as a constant guide in my life?

PRAY

Lord, help me to remember that you are with me!

3 | THE DESCENT OF THE HOLY SPIRIT

The Holy Spirit is the soul of mission.

On the day of Pentecost, the apostles were gathered in the upper room hiding and afraid. Suddenly, they were filled with the Holy Spirit and went rushing out to tell the story of Jesus so enthusiastically that those who saw them thought they were drunk. And from that moment on, they were filled with courage and conviction and never stopped proclaiming the good news. Pope Francis reminds us that in our own evangelizing efforts (which can be as small but powerful as a smile) the Spirit will guide us, keeping us from making the church some kind of exclusive club, but rather opening us all up to the joy of sharing our faith with others. There's room for everyone, and it is our duty and pleasure to invite them!

PONDER
How can I be more open and welcoming?

PRAY
Holy Spirit, fill me with your fire!

4 | THE ASSUMPTION

*Mary represents all who have faced the struggle
of life while carrying in their heart the hope
of the little and the humble.*

"My soul glories in the Lord," sings Mary in her Magnificat, and Pope Francis tells us this song is being sung all over the world, particularly in places where the body of Christ is suffering. "Wherever the cross is," the pope says, "there is hope." And it's Mary who makes this hope visible—the teenage girl chosen to be the mother of the Savior, one who in her culture would be powerless and most likely overlooked. She is the one whose song rings of the confidence that keeps us looking forward, filled with the ability to do great things for God even in our humblest actions, because God is filling these actions with his grace.

PONDER

What little thing might I do to make a difference?

PRAY

Mary, help me to say "yes" without question to God.

5 | THE CORONATION

Mary is the center of the communion of saints.

In an address on All Saints Day, Pope Francis spoke of Mary's central place in heaven, the place of honor reserved for the Mother of Jesus. Yet, the pope reminds us, this honoring of Mary as Queen of All Saints serves to highlight her humility, her obedience to what God asked of her throughout her life. Mary's experiences mirror what all humans face: her motherhood embraced joy and sorrow in equal measure, yet her answer was always "yes" to what God wanted. She gave birth to her child and watched him be killed, she lost her spouse, she became a revered elder in the new community of those who followed Jesus, and she ended her earthly life in obscurity. Her place in heaven is a sign of hope for all of us who try to serve God in all that we do.

PONDER

Which part of Mary's witness do I relate to most?

PRAY

Queen of Heaven, remind me that the humblest duties can bring great comfort to others.

More on Praying the Rosary: Spiritual Medicine

Good for the heart, for the soul, for all of life.

Pope Francis has called the Rosary "spiritual medicine," and says "it does good for the heart, for the soul, for all of life." He prays the Rosary daily, inspired by the example of Saint John Paul II, with whom he prayed the Rosary in Argentina in 1985. Remembering that occasion, Pope Francis mentioned how the prayer opened his eyes to John Paul's devotion to Our Lady. The humility of Saint John Paul's witness led Pope Francis to start praying the Rosary himself. And little by little, Pope Francis said, he lost himself in the prayer. "I was not alone," he reflected. "I was praying in the middle of the people of God."

Pope Francis' insight is worth remembering: every time we pray the Rosary, we are joining our prayer to Mary and to many others among the people of God!

If it has been a while since you prayed the Rosary, a brief refresher can be found on the following pages.

Praying The Rosary

You don't actually need rosary beads to say the Rosary, but they help free us from the distraction of having to count the Hail Marys while praying and reflecting. They also add a sense of touch to our prayer, helping us pray with our bodies as well as with our minds.

The prayer begins with the Apostles' Creed, said on the crucifix. Then an Our Father, three Hail Marys, and a Glory Be on the next beads, leading up to the medal. The next part of the prayer focuses on whichever set of Mysteries— Joyful, Sorrowful, Glorious, or Luminous—you are reflecting on while you pray. Think of the first mystery of the set (example: Joyful Mystery, the Annunciation) and pray a "decade"—an Our Father, ten Hail Marys, and a Glory Be. Follow this pattern for the other mysteries in the set. At the end of the five mysteries, the Rosary ends with the Hail, Holy Queen. Some people also end each decade with the Fatima prayer.

By custom, one set of mysteries is prayed in each Rosary. The Joyful Mysteries are prayed on Mondays and Saturdays and on the Sundays of Advent. The Sorrowful Mysteries are prayed on Tuesdays and

Fridays, and on the Sundays of Lent. The Glorious Mysteries are prayed on Wednesdays and Sundays (except in Advent and Lent). And the Luminous Mysteries are prayed on Thursdays.

But remember that there are no official rules for praying the Rosary. Don't worry about whether you have time to pray just one decade or whether you want to pray the Sorrowful Mysteries on a day when the Joyful are usually said. The important thing is to let your prayer draw you closer to Mary and Jesus.

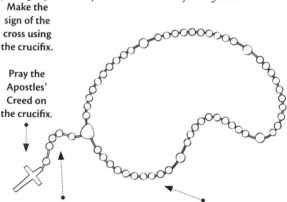

Make the sign of the cross using the crucifix.

Pray the Apostles' Creed on the crucifix.

On the introductory beads: Pray an Our Father, three Hail Marys, and a Glory Be.

For each decade, recall the mystery and pray an Our Father on the single bead, Hail Marys on the ten beads, and then a Glory Be.

Rosary Prayers

THE APOSTLES' CREED

I believe in God, the Father almighty, Creator of heaven and earth, and in Jesus Christ, his only Son, our Lord, who was conceived by the Holy Spirit, born of the Virgin Mary, suffered under Pontius Pilate, was crucified, died, and was buried; he descended into hell; on the third day he arose again from the dead; he ascended into heaven, and is seated at the right hand of God, the Father almighty; from there he will come to judge the living and the dead. I believe in the Holy Spirit, the holy catholic Church, the communion of saints, the forgiveness of sins, the resurrection of the body, and life everlasting. Amen.

THE OUR FATHER

Our Father, who art in heaven, hallowed be thy name; thy kingdom come, thy will be done on earth as it is in heaven. Give us this day our daily bread, and forgive us our trespasses, as we forgive those who trespass against us; and lead us not into temptation, but deliver us from evil. Amen.

THE HAIL MARY

Hail Mary, full of grace, the Lord is with thee: blessed art thou among women, and blessed is the fruit of thy womb, Jesus. Holy Mary, Mother of God, pray for us sinners, now and at the hour of our death. Amen.

THE GLORY BE

Glory be to the Father, and to the Son, and to the Holy Spirit. As it was in the beginning, is now, and ever shall be, world without end. Amen.

THE HAIL, HOLY QUEEN

Hail, holy Queen, Mother of Mercy; hail, our life, our sweetness and our hope. To thee do we cry, poor banished children of Eve; to thee do we send up our sighs, mourning and weeping in this valley of tears. Turn then, most gracious advocate, thine eyes of mercy towards us; and after this our exile, show unto us the blessed fruit of thy womb, Jesus; O clement, O loving, O sweet Virgin Mary. Amen.

THE FATIMA PRAYER

O my Jesus, forgive us our sins, save us from the fires of hell, and lead all souls to heaven, especially those in most need of your mercy.

FURTHER THOUGHTS

Struggle, resurrection, hope

Praying the Rosary can help us grow ever closer to Jesus and to the Blessed Virgin Mary, our mother and model of discipleship. Pondering the Rosary's mysteries while we pray helps us to deepen our faith, to reflect on how the stories of our faith connect to our own lives, and to think of how God is calling us to share his love and life with others. In all these ways, the Rosary is a great gift. Pope Francis says we should pray the Rosary often and with great attention. To do so can bring heaven and earth a little closer—especially when doing so leads us to help build the kingdom!

PONDER
Can I take the time to pray the Rosary daily?

PRAY
May these familiar prayers open my heart and soul to the service of others!